Piano/Vocal Selections

# Les Misérables

Cameron Mackintosh presents

**A Musical by
Alain Boublil & Claude-Michel Schönberg
Lyrics by Herbert Kretzmer**

**Based on the Novel by Victor Hugo**

A Cameron Mackintosh/
Royal Shakespeare Company Production

*Production credits from the first London production:*

Music by Claude-Michel Schönberg
Lyrics by Herbert Kretzmer
Original French lyrics by
Alain Boublil & Jean-Marc Natel
Additional material by James Fenton

Musical supervision and orchestrations by
John Cameron
Musical direction by Martin Koch
Sound by Andrew Bruce/Autograph
Musical staging by Kate Flatt

Costumes by Andreane Neofitou
Lighting by David Hersey
Designed by John Napier
Adapted and Directed by
Trevor Nunn & John Caird

Alain Boublil (Overseas) Limited

**Wise Publications**
London / New York / Sydney

The idea of turning *Les Misérables* into a musical came to me one evening in 1979 during a visit to London, where I had come – naturally – to see musicals.

To the French, Victor Hugo's classic novel has the status of a national monument, and I was well aware at the outset that such an enterprise would be regarded by the guardians of our heritage as an act of desecration.

Nonetheless, I discussed my idea with the composer Claude-Michel Schönberg. It seemed to both of us that here was a most exciting challenge, and a unique opportunity to work outside of the established conventions of musical theatre.

Hugo's original text lent itself very well to operatic treatment, and after nine months of hard work we had transformed the 1500-page book into an opera libretto of three acts, seven tableaux – together with a detailed description of the music and lyrics of the whole score as we then imagined it. After much revision we reached the point at which Claude-Michel could go away and start composing and I could begin work on the words. This I did – after myself deciding on the subject and title of every song – in collaboration with my friend, poet Jean-Marc Natel.

*Les Misérables* opened at the Palais des Sports in Paris in September 1980, for an eight-week season. It was extended for a further eight weeks, and would have been extended further still had it not been for other bookings. The first production was seen by over half a million people.

In 1982, Cameron Mackintosh heard the French album of *Les Misérables*, and invited Claude-Michel and I to revise our show and create an English version with James Fenton, the English poet and journalist, and directors Trevor Nunn and John Caird. Herbert Kretzmer joined us to create English counterparts of the original French lyrics, adding in the process some new lyrics specially for the English production.

*Les Misérables* opened again at the Barbican Theatre, London, on 8 October 1985. It was an instant success, and transferred on 4 December to the Palace Theatre, where it has been sold out ever since. The Broadway production opened to enormous acclaim on 12 March 1987 – *Les Misérables* the musical, like *Les Misérables* the book, has reached a worldwide audience, having played in more than twenty countries to more than twenty million people with many productions still playing and additional productions still to come.

This sheet music selection contains thirteen of our favourite songs from the London production. I hope that these words and notes somehow convey the turmoil of France in the 1820s and 30s, and especially the epic, romantic quality of those times – so vividly captured by the genius of Victor Hugo – that inspired us in our musical recreation of a literary masterpiece.

ALAIN BOUBLIL
LONDON DECEMBER 1991

# Prologue: 1815, Digne

Jean Valjean, released on parole after 19 years on the chain gang, finds that the yellow ticket-of-leave he must, by law, display condemns him to be an outcast. Only the saintly Bishop of Digne treats him kindly and Valjean, embittered by years of hardship, repays him by stealing some silver.

Valjean is caught and brought back by police, and is astonished when the Bishop lies to the police to save him, also giving him two precious candlesticks. Valjean decides to start his life anew.

## 1823, Montreuil-sur-Mer

Eight years have passed and Valjean, having broken his parole and changed his name to Monsieur Madeleine, has risen to become both a factory owner and Mayor. (No.1, 'At the End of the Day'). One of his workers, Fantine, has a secret illegitimate child. When the other women discover this, they demand her dismissal. The foreman, whose advances she has rejected, throws her out. (No.2, 'I Dreamed a Dream').

Desperate for money to pay for medicines for her daughter, Fantine sells her locket, her hair, and then joins the whores in selling herself. Utterly degraded by her new trade, she gets into a fight with a prospective customer and is about to be taken to prison by Javert when 'The Mayor' arrives and demands she be taken to hospital instead.

The Mayor then rescues a man pinned down by a runaway cart. Javert is reminded of the abnormal strength of convict 24601 Jean Valjean, a parole-breaker whom he has been tracking for years but who, he says, has just been recaptured. Valjean, unable to see an innocent man go to prison in his place, confesses to the court that he is prisoner 24601.

At the hospital, Valjean promises the dying Fantine to find and look after her daughter Cosette. Javert arrives to arrest him, but Valjean escapes.

## 1823, Montfermeil

Cosette has been lodged for five years with the Thénadiers who run an inn, horribly abusing the little girl whom they use as a skivvy while indulging their own daughter, Eponine (Nos. 3 & 4, 'Castle on a Cloud' & 'Master of the House'). Valjean finds Cosette fetching water in the dark. He pays the Thénadiers to let him take Cosette away and takes her to Paris. But Javert is still on his tail . . . (No. 5, 'Stars').

# 1832, Paris

Nine years later, there is great unrest in the city because of the likely demise of the popular leader General Lamarque, the only man left in the Government who shows any feeling for the poor. The urchin Gavroche is in his element mixing with the whores and beggars of the capital. Among the street-gangs is one led by Thénadier and his wife, which sets upon Jean Valjean and Cosette.

They are rescued by Javert, who does not recognise Valjean until after he has made good his escape. The Thénadiers' daughter Eponine, who is secretly in love with student Marius, reluctantly agrees to help him find Cosette, with whom he has fallen in love.

At a political meeting in a small café, a group of idealistic students prepares for the revolution they are sure will erupt on the death of General Lamarque. When Gavroche brings the news of the General's death, the students, led by Enjolras, stream out into the streets to whip up popular support. (No.6, 'Do You Hear the People Sing?'). Only Marius is distracted, by thoughts of the mysterious Cosette.

Cosette is consumed by thoughts of Marius, with whom she has fallen in love (Nos.7&8, 'In My Life' and 'A Heart Full of Love'). Valjean realises that his 'daughter' is changing very quickly but refuses to tell her anything of her past. In spite of her own feelings for Marius, Eponine sadly brings him to Cosette and then prevents an attempt by her father's gang to rob Valjean's house. Valjean, convinced it was Javert who was lurking outside his house, tells Cosette they must prepare to flee the country.

On the eve of the revolution, the students and Javert see the situation from their different viewpoints; Cosette and Marius part in despair of ever meeting again; Eponine mourns the loss of Marius; and Valjean looks forward to the security of exile. The Thénadiers, meanwhile, dream of rich pickings underground from the chaos to come.

The students prepare to build the barricade. Marius, noticing that Eponine has joined the insurrection, sends her with a letter to Cosette, which is intercepted at the Rue Plumet by Valjean. Eponine decides, despite what he has said to her, to rejoin Marius at the Barricade. (No.9, 'On My Own').

The barricade is built and the revolutionaries defy an army warning that they must give up or die. Gavroche exposes Javert as a police spy. In trying to return to the barricade, Eponine is shot and killed. (No.10, 'A Little Fall of Rain'). Valjean arrives at the barricades in search of Marius. He is given the chance to kill Javert but instead lets him go.

The students settle down for a night on the barricade (No.11, 'Drink with Me') and in the quiet of the night, Valjean prays to God to save Marius from the onslaught which is to come (No.12 'Bring Him Home'). The next day, with ammunition running low, Gavroche runs out to collect more and is shot. The rebels are all killed, including their leader Enjolras.

Valjean escapes into the sewers with the unconscious Marius. After meeting Thénadier, who is robbing the corpses of the rebels, he emerges into the light only to meet Javert once more. He pleads for time to deliver the young man to hospital. Javert decides to let him go and, his unbending principles of justice shattered by Valjean's own mercy, he kills himself by throwing himself into the swollen River Seine.

A few months later, Marius, unaware of the identity of his rescuer, has recovered and recalls, at Cosette's side, the days of the barricade where all his friends have lost their lives. (No.13, 'Empty Chairs at Empty Tables'). Valjean confesses the truth of his past to Marius and insists that after the young couple are married, he must go away rather than taint the sanctity and safety of their union.

At Marius and Cosette's wedding, the Thénadiers try to blackmail Marius. Thénadier says Cosette's 'father' is a murderer and as proof produces a ring which he stole from the corpse in the sewers the night the barricades fell. It is Marius' own ring and he realises it was Valjean who rescued him that night. He and Cosette go to Valjean where Cosette learns for the first time of her own history before the old man dies, joining the spirits of Fantine, Eponine and all those who died on the barricades.

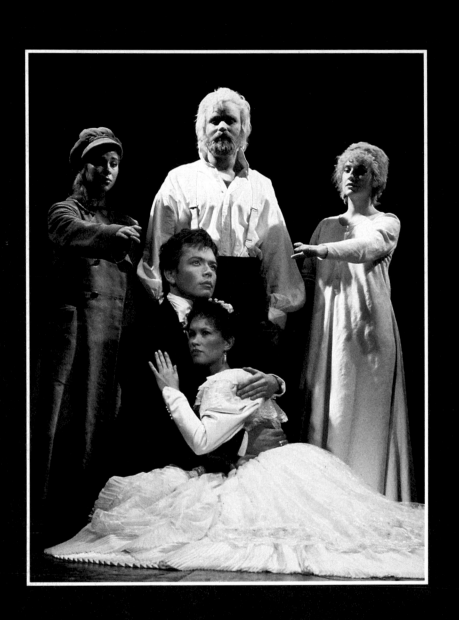

# At the End of the Day

Music by CLAUDE-MICHEL SCHÖNBERG
Lyrics by HERBERT KRETZMER.
Original French lyrics by ALAIN BOUBLIL & JEAN-MARC NATEL.

# I Dreamed a Dream

Music by CLAUDE-MICHEL SCHÖNBERG
Lyrics by HERBERT KRETZMER.
Original French lyrics by ALAIN BOUBLIL & JEAN-MARC NATEL.

I dreamed a dream in time gone by
Then I was young and un - a - fraid

When hope was high and life worth
When dreams were made and used and

li - ving.____
wa - sted.____

I dreamed that love would ne - ver die,
There was no ran - som to be paid,

I dreamed that God would be for - giv - ing.____
No song un - sung, no wine un - tast - ed.____

# Castle on a Cloud

Music by CLAUDE-MICHEL SCHÖNBERG
Lyrics by HERBERT KRETZMER.
Original French lyrics by ALAIN BOUBLIL & JEAN-MARC NATEL.

# Master of the House

Music by CLAUDE-MICHEL SCHÖNBERG
Lyrics by HERBERT KRETZMER.
Original French lyrics by ALAIN BOUBLIL & JEAN-MARC NATEL.

Glad to do my friends a fa-vour _____ Does-n't cost me to be nice but
Re-si-dents are more than wel - come _____ Bri-dal suite is oc-cu-pied! _____

no-thing gets you no-thing Ev - 'ry-thing has got a lit-tle price! _____
Rea-son-a-ble charg-es Plus _____ some lit-tle ex-tra on the side! _____

Mas-ter of the House Keep-er of the zoo Rea-dy to re-lieve them of a
Charge 'em for the lice Ex-tra for the mice Two per-cent for look-ing in the

sou, or two. Wa-ter-ing the wine Ma-king up the weight Pick-ing up their knick-knacks When they
mir-ror twice! Here a lit-tle slice There a lit-tle cut Three percent for sleep-ing with the

# Stars

Music by CLAUDE-MICHEL SCHÖNBERG
Lyrics by HERBET KRETZMER & ALAIN BOUBLIL.

# Do You Hear the People Sing?

Music by CLAUDE-MICHEL SCHÖNBERG
Lyrics by HERBERT KRETZMER.
Original French lyrics by ALAIN BOUBLIL & JEAN-MARC NATEL.

# In My Life

Music by CLAUDE-MICHEL SCHÖNBERG
Lyrics by HERBERT KRETZMER.
Original French lyrics by ALAIN BOUBLIL & JEAN-MARC NATEL.

# A Heart Full of Love

Music by CLAUDE-MICHEL SCHÖNBERG
Lyrics by HERBERT KRETZMER.
Original French lyrics by ALAIN BOUBLIL & JEAN-MARC NATEL.

# On My Own

Music by CLAUDE-MICHEL SCHÖNBERG
Lyrics by HERBERT KRETZMER, ALAIN BOUBLIL, JOHN CAIRD,
TREVOR NUNN & JEAN-MARC NATEL.

# A Little Fall of Rain

Music by CLAUDE-MICHEL SCHÖNBERG.
Lyrics by HERBERT KRETZMER.
Original French lyrics by ALAIN BOUBLIL & JEAN-MARC NATEL.

# Drink with Me

Music by CLAUDE-MICHEL SCHÖNBERG
Lyrics by ALAIN BOUBLIL & HERBERT KRETZMER.

Drink with me to days_____ gone by._____ Sing with
me to days_____ gone by _____ To the

me the songs_____ we knew_____ Here's to pret - ty girls Who
life that used_____ to be _____ At the shrine of friend - ship

went to our heads Here's to wit - ty girls Who went to our beds Here's to
Ne - ver say die! Let the wine of friend - ship Ne - ver run dry. Here's to

them And here's_____ to you!_____ Drink with
you. And here's

# Bring Him Home

Music by CLAUDE-MICHEL SCHÖNBERG
Lyrics by HERBERT KRETZMER & ALAIN BOUBLIL.

2.  Bring him peace
    Bring him joy
    He is young. He is only a boy.
    You can take. You can give.
    Let him be. Let him live.
    If I die, let me die.
    Let him live. Bring him home
    Bring him home
    Bring him home.

# Empty Chairs at Empty Tables

Music by CLAUDE-MICHEL SCHÖNBERG
Lyrics by HERBERT KRETZMER & ALAIN BOUBLIL.

**Andante** (♩ = 88)

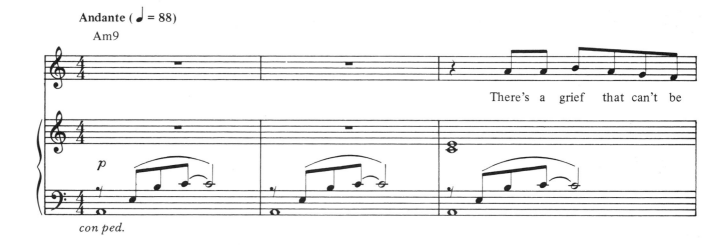

There's a grief that can't be

spo-ken ____ There's a pain goes on and on ____

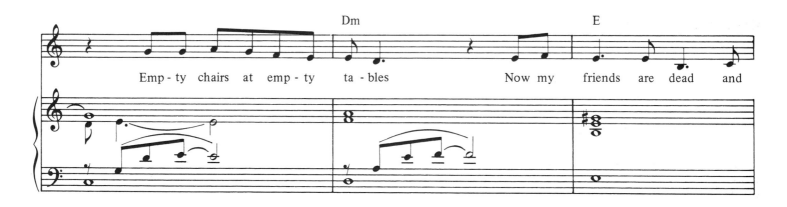

Emp-ty chairs at emp-ty ta-bles Now my friends are dead and

gone. Here they talked of re-vo-lu-tion